"Eh...Jesus... Yes, Peter...?"

CONTENTS

John Bell and Graham Maule are members of the Iona Community and lead the Wild Goose Worship Group. It is to the members of the group, who have inspired so much and so many, that this collection of scripts is fondly dedicated.

First Published 1987

The wild goose is a Celtic symbol of the Holy Spirit.
It serves as the logo of Iona Community Publications.

© Copyright 1987 The Iona Community   ISBN 0 947988 20 3
Printed by Wild Goose Publications

The Publishing Division of the Iona Community
Pearce Institute, 840 Govan Road, Glasgow G51 3UT
Tel: 041 − 445 4561

The Call

(THE TWO CHARACTERS STAND APART FROM EACH OTHER,
PETER LOOKING QUITE ABSORBED IN HIMSELF)

JESUS : Peter . . . ?

PETER : Yes, Jesus . . .?

JESUS : Come with me.

PETER : Where are you going?

JESUS : I'm not telling you.

PETER : Do you not know?

JESUS : Oh yes, I've a fair idea.

PETER : Then . . . why won't you tell me?

JESUS : You might not like it.

PETER : Well, thanks for your consideration, Jesus.

(A PAUSE)

JESUS : Peter . . . ?

PETER : Yes, Jesus . . . ?

JESUS : Come with me.

PETER : Can I bring somebody else?

JESUS : Just bring yourself.

PETER : Will there only be the two of us?

JESUS : Oh no, there'll be plenty of others.

PETER : Will I know some of them?
. . . what about my cousin Alec . . . will he be there?
and is there any chance of my sister coming if she still fancies
you?

. . . and what about my grannie?
Oh, Jesus, I'd love to bring my grannie to meet you . . .
Can I?

JESUS : Peter . . . just bring yourself.

PETER : But . . . but . . . you said there would be others.

JESUS : That's right.

PETER : Who are they?

JESUS : I'm not telling you.

PETER : Why not?

JESUS : You might not like them.

PETER : Aw, thanks a bunch, Jesus!

(A PAUSE)

JESUS : Peter . . . ?

PETER : Yes, Jesus???

JESUS : Come with me.

PETER : Jesus, I've got better things to do than go on a mystery tour.
But I'll think about it.
Just tell me what I'll need.

JESUS : What do you mean?

PETER : Well, if I'm going somewhere I don't know, with people you
refuse to tell me about, there are some things that might come
in very handy.

JESUS : Like what?

PETER : Like something to read in case I get bored . . . .
Like something to sing in case I get sad . . . .

Like a new pair of jeans in case there's a dance or a party.

JESUS : Peter, you'll not need anything.
Just bring yourself.
That's enough to contend with.

PETER : Jesus . . . do you want me to end up like you???

JESUS : Peter . . .
I'm going . . .

Are you coming with me?

* * * * * * *

4

The Silver Coin

PETER : Eh . . . Jesus . . . ?

JESUS : Yes, Peter . . . ?

PETER : Eh . . . I've got . . . eh . . . we've got . . .
Eh . . .
I think there's a problem!

JESUS : Yes, Peter?

PETER : It's a problem about money.

JESUS : I see . . . . so what's the problem?

PETER : Eh . . . we don't have any.

JESUS : But that's nothing new, Peter.

PETER : No, Jesus.

(A PAUSE)

PETER : Eh . . . Jesus?

JESUS : Yes, Peter?

PETER : What do you think about taxes?

JESUS : I've never been in one, Peter.

PETER : No . . . not tax**is** . . . tax**es**!

JESUS : Well, what do you think about them?

PETER : I worry when we don't have money to pay them . . . .
That's the problem . . .
We're going to Capernaum . . .
When we get there, they'll ask us to pay taxes . . .
And that means money . . . and . . .
And we don't have any.

JESUS : But that's nothing new, Peter.

PETER : No, Jesus.

(A PAUSE)

PETER : Eh . . . Jesus?

JESUS : (GETTING EXASPERATED) Yes, Peter! !

PETER : What are you going to do then?

5

JESUS : What am **I** going to do then?
You mean, what are **you** going to do then!

PETER : Yes . . . I mean, what are **you** going to do then . . . .
I mean . . . what am **I** going to do then.

JESUS : You're going to stop worrying . . .
. . . and start fishing.

PETER : Fishing???

JESUS : That's right.

You're going to take a line and throw it in the lake.
And when you pull it out, you'll find you've caught
a big fish . . .
. . . . . with a silver coin in its mouth.

PETER : Jesus, I've heard of gold fillings . . .
But this is ridiculous!

How could a fish have a silver coin in its mouth?

JESUS : Oh, it'll get one . . .
When you take it to the market . . .

It's amazing how much some folk will give for a 5lb. salmon.

PETER : Oh, I see.

JESUS : Had you not thought of that?

PETER : No, Jesus, I didn't think.

JESUS : But that's nothing new, Peter.

PETER : No, Jesus.

*   *   *   *   *   *   *

6

Being Serious

PETER : Jesus...?

JESUS : Yes, Peter...?

PETER : Why are you not like Moses?

JESUS : You've seen Moses, have you?

PETER : No... but I've read the book...
and it's quite obvious that there's a major difference
between him and you.

JESUS : Could it be that he had a stammer?

PETER : No, no... it's just...
It's just that he asked us to do easy things.

JESUS : Peter, I'm not sure you have read the book.
What do you mean by easy things?

PETER : Well, for example... he says "honour your father and mother".

JESUS : And you find that easy?

PETER : Listen, Jesus, I used to think that my parents were hard to get
on with. But after living with my in-laws for four years, I think
they're saints in comparison. I'd honour them any day.

JESUS : I see... that's one example.

PETER : Oh, there are plenty of others. Moses told us that we should not
covet our neighbour's wife.

JESUS : And you find that commandment easy to keep?

PETER : Come on, Jesus... you've seen Mrs. Cohen.

JESUS : Oh yes, she... eh... no comment.

PETER : You see... what Moses asks is quite reasonable.
What you ask is quite outrageous.

I mean... just take a small example...
Were you serious when you said that if someone slapped us on
the right cheek we should offer the left as well?
Do you want us all to end up looking like bloated pomegranites
every time there's an argument?

JESUS : Would you rather that it was an eye for an eye and a tooth for a
tooth and everyone ended up blind and gumsy?

PETER :	No . . . I suppose not. . . . eh . . . were you serious when you said that we should lend and not ask for repayment?
JESUS :	Why?
PETER :	It's just that . . . eh . . . I payed your temple tax for you a couple of months ago.
JESUS :	Oh, I meant what I said, Peter!
PETER :	And did you mean it when you said, "don't cut the hair at the sides of your head or trim your beard"?
JESUS :	I didn't say that, Peter, Moses did.
PETER :	Oh . . . so you've read the book too. What about loving your enemy?
JESUS :	What about loving your enemy?
PETER :	Jesus, I'd find it easier to covet Mrs. Cohen than I would to love my enemy. You've seen Mrs. Cohen, but you haven't seen the people I call my enemies. It's not easy to love them, Jesus. It's not easy to do what you ask us to do.
JESUS :	I never said it would be easy, Peter, ... I said it would be different. Just as I never said I would be the answer, I said I was the way.
PETER :	But when you said that one day you would come back and take us to yourself; And when you told us you would be with us to the end of the world . . . Did you mean what you said? Were you serious?
JESUS :	Peter, I can't come again to you unless I first go away, and I can't be with you to the end of the world unless I live not just in time, but in eternity. Often when you have asked me questions, I have given you no straight answer, I've just posed another question for you to think about. But when you ask me if I'm serious about the things I say; If you ask me if I'm serious about the promises I make; If you ask me if I mean what I command you, outrageous though it may be, then my answer to you is straight. It is "yes". What's your answer to me?

*   *   *   *   *   *   *

8

A Simple Question

PETER : Eh ... Jesus ... ?

JESUS : Yes, Peter ... ?

PETER : Eh ... can I ask you a simple question?

JESUS : As long as you don't expect a simple answer.

PETER : Eh ... well, it's about a certain statement you made the other day, much to the displeasure of certain people.

JESUS : Would these 'certain people' wander about the Galilean countryside with only a stick and one set of clothing?

PETER : Eh ... perhaps ...

JESUS : So, I've upset the disciples again .. eh?

PETER : Well ... I'm not one for gossip.

JESUS : All right, what did I say?

PETER : You said we've to become like children!

JESUS : You were listening, Peter ...

PETER : More than that, you said we wouldn't get into the Kingdom unless we became like little children.

JESUS : So?

PETER : So ... what did you mean?

JESUS : Well, Peter, how would you describe children?

PETER : Eh ... they're naive ... innocent .... harmless, I suppose. ... oh, and a bit wet sometimes!

JESUS : ... innocent, harmless, wet ...
Peter, how many kids do you have?

PETER : Jesus, thanks to you I haven't seen my wife for three years. But at the last count, we didn't have any.

JESUS : Then the quicker you have some, the better. You'll soon find out that they're not innocent, naive or harmless. Anyone who thinks differently must have nappies over their eyes.

PETER : So, what are they like?

JESUS : Use your memory, Peter. Think of the children we've met.

9

PETER : We haven't met any.

JESUS : What about the ones in the temple . . . ?

PETER : Jesus, they sounded like the cats' choir and you had the cheek to say they were "perfecting God's praise".

JESUS : Peter, our musical tastes may differ, but I don't think you can deny that they were really happy.

PETER : Not like the Pharisees . . . eh, Jesus?

JESUS : Not like the Pharisees, and not like a lot of adults who think that God's only pleased when you look as delirious as an undertaker's dummy.

PETER : So, we've to be happy. Anything else?

JESUS : Think of a girl, Peter . . . Jairus's daughter.
What do you remember of her?

PETER : Now if ever there was an undertaker's dummy . . .

JESUS : That's right. But she trusted me.
I said "get up" and she got up.
How many adults take me at my word . . . including a certain company of ex-civil servants and fishermen?

PETER : So, we've to be happy and trustful. Is that it?

JESUS : Peter, use your memory a bit more. Think of a field . . .
5000 people . . . what shall we give them to eat???

PETER : Oh, you mean the wee boy I brought to you.

JESUS : Peter, where is your memory? Andrew brought the wee boy.
You just stood and giggled. But what quality did the wee boy show?
. . . it begins with a 'G' . . .

PETER : Eh . . . generosity?

JESUS : Peter, you should try crosswords.

PETER : So, to be like children we should be happy, trustful and generous.

JESUS : There's something else.

PETER : There always is!

JESUS : Do you remember the crowd of men who surrounded me wanting to ask me very intellectual questions . . . . Do you remember who came through the crowd?

PETER : You don't mean the wee lassie with jam on her face?

JESUS : I most certainly do.

PETER : Do we have to get jam on our face to get into the kingdom of heaven?

JESUS : No.
But think of what her mother said when she came to take her back. She was all apologetic.
She said, "I'm sorry, mister, she's awful curious".

PETER : Jesus, is curiosity one of the things we should learn from children?

JESUS : Yes.

PETER : So a certain ex fisherman who wanders around Galilee with only a stick and one set of clothing might just have a toe in the kingdom?

JESUS : With all the questions you ask, Peter, you don't have a toe in the kingdom.
You're up to your neck in it!

* * * * * * *

A New Experience

PETER : Eh . . . Jesus . . . ?

JESUS : Yes, Peter . . . ?

PETER : Eh . . . I was just thinking . . .

JESUS : Is that a new experience, Peter?

PETER : I was just thinking about this . . . eh . . . church.

JESUS : Which church, Peter?

PETER : The one . . . the one you're going to build . . . on me.

JESUS : Oh, that church.
Well, what were you thinking?

PETER : Eh . . . I was thinking that I'm not exactly the world's best administrator.

JESUS : There are some people who would say that you weren't exactly the world's best fisherman.

PETER : Oh, Jesus . . . you said you wouldn't mention that again!

JESUS : Sorry, Peter.
Now . . . you were saying . . .

PETER : I was saying that I'm not the world's best administrator and you haven't exactly given me much of a clue as to what I should do.

JESUS : What do you mean?

PETER : Well, for example . . . who is the church for?
Is it just for the Jews?

JESUS : No.

PETER : Is it just for Gentiles?

JESUS : No.

PETER : Is it for everybody?

JESUS : Mm . . hm . .

PETER : Including women???

JESUS : Mm . . hm . .

PETER : Jesus!!!

JESUS : Yes, Peter ... ?

PETER : Do you know what you're letting yourself in for?
I mean,
Do you know what you're letting **me** in for?

JESUS : Do you have something against women?

PETER : No, I'm married to one.
But, I mean, in the synagogue they know their place.

JESUS : I thought we were talking about the church.

PETER : Exactly!
If they don't know their place in the church, they'll ruin
everything.

JESUS : You mean they might get things organised?

PETER : Well ... yes ...

JESUS : And that would be a new experience ... wouldn't it?

PETER : Well .... well ...
Look, quite apart from the women, what do you want the men to
do?

Do you want us to sing .... standing up or sitting down?
Do you want us to kneel to pray, or stretch our hands in the air?
Do you want candles and incense ... or has the church to be a
smokeless zone?

Are there to be speakers or silence?
Do you want drums and trumpets?
I mean, Thomas suggested guitars, but I told him that guitars
gave God a sore head.

JESUS : What gave you that impression?

PETER : Amos 5, verse 23 .... remember?

JESUS : Oh ... of course ...

PETER : And another thing, Jesus ... how do you want it run?

JESUS : Are you talking about a marathon, Peter?

PETER : No .. the church .... how do you want it run?

James says it should be a territorial democracy.
Andrew thought it might be a centralised bureaucracy.
Simon said that people should do as they please ... but he's just
an anarchist!

What do you say?

JESUS : Not very much.

PETER : Jesus, be serious.
I mean . . . you said that you were going to build the church on me, but you don't give me a clue as to what it should be like.

What happens if you disappear and I drop dead?
Will the whole thing go up in a puff of smoke?

JESUS : Well, that would be an interesting way of finding your successor.

PETER : Pardon?

JESUS : Peter, Peter,
Don't worry about the church.
That's God's problem, not yours.
You set your eyes on the kingdom and God will make clear what should be the shape of the church.

For God wants the church to be the servant of the kingdom, not the master,
to celebrate the kingdom, not to dominate it,
to be a sign of the good news, not just a reminder of the bad.
(PAUSE)

PETER : Jesus . . . I don't think you've answered any of my questions.

JESUS : Is that a new experience, Peter?

PETER : No, Jesus.

            *   *   *   *   *   *   *

Set Apart

PETER : Eh ... Jesus ... ?

JESUS : Yes, Peter ... ?

PETER : Do you mind if I ask you a personal question?

JESUS : I haven't got a penny on me, Peter.

PETER : No, it's not about money.

JESUS : Then what is it about?

PETER : It's just .... eh .... it's just ...
Eh ... are you ... you know ... 'ordained'?

JESUS : Am I ... you know ... 'ordained'?
What do you mean?

PETER : Well, have you had hands laid on you?

JESUS : My mother used to clip my ear when I was a boy.
Does that count?

PETER : No! ... I mean have you been 'set apart'?

JESUS : Oh, regularly.
The Pharisees do it every time I go near them.

PETER : Jesus, do you know what I'm talking about?

JESUS : Yes.
Yes, I do know what you're talking about.
But why are you asking me the question?

PETER : Just because everybody who's special in God's eyes seems to
have been ordained.

JESUS : Like who?

PETER : Well ... like Abraham, I suppose.

JESUS : Eh ... Peter ... Abraham wasn't ordained.
He just stopped enjoying his retirement and started travelling.

PETER : What about his wife?

JESUS : You mean Sarah? She became pregnant.
That's not the same as becoming ordained.

PETER : What about David? Did he not get ordained?

JESUS : No, he got crowned.
And that's not the same.

15

PETER : . . . just like getting pregnant.

JESUS : No. A pregnancy and a coronation are entirely different.

PETER : Oh, Jesus, I know that.
My mother had four confinements.
She'd rather have a coronation any day.

JESUS : Never mind your mother. Who else do you think was ordained?

PETER : Eh . . . Daniel.

JESUS : No. He was a diplomat who was good with dangerous animals.

PETER : What about Amos?

JESUS : No. He was a shepherd who was good with words.

PETER : Well, Jeremiah then.

JESUS : No. He was an eccentric who was good for an argument.

PETER : Jesus, surely some famous folk got ordained?

JESUS : Oh yes.
Some did.
There have always been priests ordained and set apart to attend to the mysteries of the faith.

But there also have been prophets and pioneers, many unordained, whose job it has been to demonstrate the will of God in places where the priests made no impact.

PETER : So, is it important to be ordained?

JESUS : Peter, the day will come when, because you are neither a priest nor a prophet, you will be sneered at and sent to where you would rather avoid.

People will look at you and the others who follow me.
And they'll ridicule you for being 'untrained laymen'.
You will then wish you were a priest or prophet, set apart or set aside, made and meant to be special.

But what really matters is not to be seen as special but to be seen as faithful to the one who has chosen you.

(PAUSE)

PETER : So you do not want me to become a rabbi or a father or a reverend?

JESUS : Peter, I want you to be my disciple.
Anything else is second place.
Anything less is second best.

*　　*　　*　　*　　*　　*　　*

16

The Keys

(JESUS AND PETER STAND AT THE GATES OF HEAVEN)

PETER :   Eh . . . Jesus . . . ?

JESUS :   Yes, Peter . . . ?

PETER :   Eh . . . I've got something to tell you.

JESUS :   Well, what is it?

PETER :   Eh . . . I think I've lost the keys.

JESUS :   You think you've what???

PETER :   I . . . I think I've lost the keys.

JESUS :   Where did you see them last?

PETER :   I think I left them in the door.

JESUS :   (PRODUCING KEYS) Are these them by any chance?

PETER :   Oh, Jesus, thank goodness for that.
           Where did you find them?

JESUS :   I found them where you left them . . . in the door.

PETER :   But what were you doing at the door?

JESUS :   Oh, I thought I'd just nip outside for a wee while and look at the
           new arrivals.

PETER :   Did they recognise you?

JESUS :   Peter, did they ever?
           No. In any case the new arrivals always expect that everybody
           here will be dressed in golden wings and a white nightgown.

           So, before I went out, I changed into a kilt and turban.

PETER :   You what???

JESUS :   No. I'm just kidding. I went the way I'm dressed just now.
           But nobody recognised me, even though I knew them all.
           And their faces when they got near the pearly gates . . . .

PETER :   Oh don't tell me. Gabriel and I have a great time guessing who's
           who when they come to the door.

JESUS :   Guessing who's who?

PETER : Well, guessing who's what . . . or who was what.

JESUS : I'm not any clearer.

PETER : Well, for example, when Presbyterians come . . . I mean when ex-Presbyterians come . . . and you greet them with a smile, they think there's something wrong. You would think they expected heaven to be a painful place.
And they can't understand why David sings *Psalm 23* to a Jewish tune. They seem to imagine that he wrote *Crimond* as well as the words.

That's the men. The women are entirely different. Whenever you open the door to Presbyterian women they try to sell you a ticket for a coffee morning.

JESUS : What about the Catholics?

PETER : Oh, you always know when the Catholics have arrived. They're hardly in the door but they're asking for your mother.

JESUS : Aye, she's got a great fan club.

PETER : Then, of course, you get the Orangemen marching up to the gates singing the sash and just about swallowing their tonsils when they see John 23rd out cutting the grass.

And you can recognise the ministers and priests right away.
And they try to speak to you in New Testament Greek.
Have you ever heard an Irish priest trying to say "I'm Father Seamus O'Brien from Cork" in Greek?

JESUS : I can't say I have. But, Peter, you've only mentioned Europeans.

PETER : Maybe so I have.
I suppose that's because many of the Africans and Asians, especially from the poor parts of the world don't find heaven so strange. It's as if they've glimpsed it on earth.

(A PAUSE)
It's the poor and despised and the forgotten who I most like to welcome, Jesus . . .
. . . the ones who were ignored or turned off by the church, but who still remembered you . . .
. . . the ones who looked down all the time they were on earth, because nobody ever said, "look up", nobody ever said, "you're important", . . . nobody ever touched them or listened to their story.

(PAUSE)

18

JESUS : I know what you mean.

I met a woman like that the other day.
She was a widow.
She had once done something wrong in her early days.
And though I had forgiven her, nobody else did.

I looked at her eyes and remembered all the people who had made her cry.
I looked at her hands and remembered all the good work she had done which no one had thanked her for.
I looked into her heart and remembered how it had been broken and yet how it had cared and loved.

And I said to her, "Bessie, there's some people here I'd like you to meet".

And I was just about to introduce her to Martha and Lazarus, when she took my hand and said,

"Jesus, I've had three surprises since I came to heaven.

The first was finding all the people who are here.

The second was finding all the people who are'nt here.

And the third surprise was finding that I was here myself".

(PAUSE)

PETER : Well . . . of such is the kingdom . . . eh?

JESUS : Yes . . . of such is the kingdom.

(A PAUSE)
Here, Peter, I'll better be getting back to the top table.
I'll see you later.

PETER : Eh . . . Jesus . . . the keys?

JESUS : (TAKES THEM TO HIM) Sorry, Peter.

PETER : Thank you, Jesus.

* * * * * * *

19

CURRENT PUBLICATIONS OF THE IONA COMMUNITY

SONGS OF THE INCARNATION   ISBN 0 950135186
      John Bell & Graham Maule

THE IONA COMMUNITY WORSHIP BOOK   ISBN 0 950135194
      Iona Abbey

THROUGH WOOD AND NAILS   Record No.146/REC/S

THROUGH WOOD AND NAILS   Cassette No.IC/WGP/001
      Iona Abbey

THE WHOLE EARTH SHALL CRY GLORY   Paperback   ISBN 0 947988 00 9

THE WHOLE EARTH SHALL CRY GLORY   Hardback   ISBN 0 947988 04 1
      Rev. George F. MacLeod

WILD GOOSE PRINTS No.1   ISBN 0 947988 06 8
      John Bell & Graham Maule

WHAT IS THE IONA COMMUNITY?   ISBN 0 947988 07 6

WOMEN'S WORDS FROM IONA ABBEY   ISBN 0 947988 08 4
      Kathryn Galloway

A TOUCHING PLACE   Cassette No.IC/WGP/004
      Wild Goose Worship Group

A TOUCHING PLACE   ISBN 0 947988 09 2
      John Bell & Graham Maule

WILD GOOSE PRINTS No.2   ISBN 0 947988 10 6
      John Bell & Graham Maule

COLUMBA – The Man & The Myth   ISBN 0 947988 11 4
      Mitchell Bunting

IN PRAISE OF GOD'S GOODNESS   ISBN 0 947988 12 2
      Kathryn Galloway

THE IONA PILGRIMAGE   ISBN 0 947988 13 0
      Jack Kellet

A CHILD'S STORY   ISBN 0 947988 14 9
      Caroline & Maddy Clarke

FOLLY AND LOVE   Cassette No.IC/WGP/005

FOLLY AND LOVE   ISBN 0 947988 15 7
      Iona Abbey

SINGING THE SACRAMENT   ISBN 0 947988 16 5
      John Bell

90 RECIPES FROM THE IONA COMMUNITY   ISBN 0 947988 17 3
      Sue Pattison

APOCALYPSE SOON?   ISBN 0 947988 18 1
      Alan E. Lewis

GRACE AND DYSENTERY   ISBN 0 947988 19 X
      Ron Ferguson

EH...JESUS...YES, PETER...?   ISBN 0 947988 20 3
      John Bell & Graham Maule

FREEDOM IS COMING   Cassette No.IC/WGP/006

FREEDOM IS COMING   ISBN 91 86788 15 7
      Utryck

CLOTH FOR THE CRADLE   Cassette No.IC/WGP/007
      Wild Goose Worship Group

Other publications are in preparation, Please ask for details